Harry Potter

Exciting Quiz

The 400 Newest & Updated Quiz

Questions & Answers

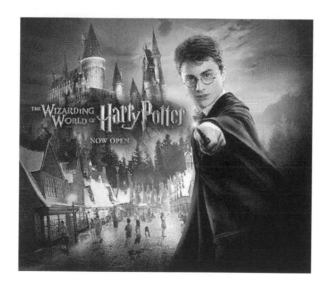

By Jason Smith

Harry Potter Overview

Harry Potter was first made into a movie in 2001, with *Harry Potter and the Philosopher Stone*, and continues to fascinate fans. It has been around since the 1990s when J.K. Rowling wrote the first novel. Harry Potter and the Philosopher with lots of precious details and perfect complementary humor that J.K. Rowling storms the timeless classic. Now it has spawned the spin-off that fans love. However, have you mastered the secrets of J.K. Rowling's seven magical books? In this book, you will find a better way to be as knowledgeable as Hermione in a Transfiguration class or whether your head is bare and full of air, dead flies, and fluff bits. This Nastily Exhausting Wizard Trivia will thoroughly test your proficiency and assess, once and for all, whether you're a real "Harry Potter," expert.

I scoured **Harry Potter and the Sorcerer's Stone** to answer questions in the categories of easy, medium and challenging. They are the perfect way for you to have some fun while learning the background of spells, creatures, Hogwarts, and more. They also provide general knowledge of Harry Potter and his Hogwarts journey. The Harry Potter series continues to inspire readers of all ages with its universal themes of friendship, imagination, and the triumph of good over bad.

Part 1: Question 1-15

1. What is Dumbledore's first name?

2. What is the last name of the family Harry Potter lives with at the beginning of the story?

3. When the story starts, where was Harry's room at the Dursley's located?

4. When Harry visited the zoo on Dudley's birthday, which animal did he end up talking to?

5. Which birthday does Harry begin in a shack on a rock in the middle of the water?

6. What does Hagrid give Harry for his eleventh birthday?

7. Who was the first person to tell Harry he was a wizard?

8. What is a Muggle?

9. What did Hagrid add to Dudley Dursley's back end?

10. What is the name of the bank the wizards use?

11. What is the name of the wizarding newspaper?

12. What is Hermione's last name?

13. What was the name of Harry's first Defense Against the Dark Arts teacher?

14. What's the name of the hidden place which has shops for robes, telescopes, and wands?

15. What is the name of Harry's owl?

Part 1: Answer 1-15

1. Albus

2. Dursley

3. Under the stairs

4. A snake

5. Eleventh

6. A cake

7. Hagrid

8. A person who can't do magic

9. A pig's tail

10. Gringotts

11. The Daily Prophet

12. Granger

13. Professor Quirrell

14. Diagon Alley

15. Hedwin

Part 2: Question 16-31

16. What is remarkable about the wand that chose Harry Potter?

17. What is the name of the train station in which a person can board The Hogwarts Express?

18. What is Ron's last name?

19. Which house is Hermione in?

20. Which house is Draco Malfoy in?

21. Where does Harry Potter first meet Hermione?

22. Was Hagrid ever a student at Hogwarts?

23. What is the name of Filch's cat?

24. What is the name of the Hogwarts Herbology teacher?

25. What is Neville's last name?

26. Which professor is the head of Slytherin house?

27. What does a Remembrall do when you've forgotten something?

28. Which wizarding skill can Harry do best when he first enters Hogwarts?

29. Who is Harry chasing when he first flies a broom?

30. What position does Harry Potter play on Gryffindor's Quidditch team?

31. Which position on a Quidditch team tries to keep the opposing team from getting the Quaffle through the hoops?

Part 2: Answer 16-31

16. It is the same materials as   Voldemort's

17. King's Cross Station

18. Weasley

19. Gryffindor

20. Slytherin

21. On the train

22. Yes (but he got expelled)

23. Mrs. Norris

24. Professor Sprout

25. Longbottom

26. Professor Snape

27. It glows red

28. Flying on a broom

29. Draco

30. Seeker

31. Keeper

Part 3: Question 32-47

32. Which position on a Quidditch team tries to get the Golden Snitch?

33. How many points are scored if a Seeker catches the Golden Snitch?

34. Which animals fly in the Great Hall on Halloween?

35. When Harry Potter first attends Hogwarts, who is the boys' Prefect for Gryffindor?

36. When did Harry, Ron, and Hermione finally become friends?

37. What color Quidditch robes does Gryffindor wear?

38. Whom did Ron and Hermione first believe was jinxing Harry's broom at his first Quidditch match?

39. What is the 3-headed dog's name?

40. What kind of cloak did Harry get as a present his first Christmas at Hogwarts?

41. Whom did Harry see in the Mirror of Erised?

42. What does the Elixir of Life do to a person who drinks it?

43. How did Harry and Hermione get a dragon to the tallest tower of Hogwarts without being seen?

44. Which half-man, half-horse creature did Harry meet in the forest?

45. Something is wounded in the forest, spilling silvery blood. What is it?

46. What is the name of You-Know-Who?

47. How do you calm down Fluffy, the three-headed dog?

Part 3: Answer 32-47

32. Seeker

33. 150

34. Bats

35. Percy Weasley

36. After the battle with the troll

37. Red (scarlet)

38. Snape

39. Fluffy

40. Invisibility Cloak

41. His parents

42. Makes them immortal

43. They used the invisibility cloak

44. A centaur

45. A unicorn

46. Voldemort (also, Tom Riddle)

47. Play it some music

Part 4: Question 48-59

48. Harry thought he saw birds on the way to the Sorcerer's stone. What did they turn out to be instead?

49. Which character is the youngest seeker in a century?

50. Which game does Ron direct when he, Harry, and Hermione are on their way to the Sorcerer's stone?

51. Who was actually muttering a spell trying to knock Harry Potter off his broom in his first Quidditch match?

52. What is the name of Ron's rat?

53. Who let the troll in to Hogwarts?

54. Where was Voldemort's face the first time Harry Potter saw it?

54. On the back of Quirrell's head

55. What happened to Quirrell's hands when he tried to seize Harry Potter?

56. Who said, "Fear of a name increases fear of the thing itself"?

57. Which Hogwarts student had the Invisibility Cloak before Dumbledore gave it to Harry?

57. Harry's father

58. Which house won the House Cup at the end of the first book?

59. Who had the best grades of all the first-year students?

Part 4: Answer 48-59

48. Flying keys

49. Harry Potter

50. Chess

51. Professor Quirrell

52. Scabbers

53. Professor Quirrell

55. They burned

56. Dumbledore

58. Gryffindor

59. Hermione

Part 5: Question 60-70

60. Are Hogwarts students allowed to use magic during their summer breaks?

61. What is the golden snitch?

62. What is the yule ball?

63. What are the death eaters?

64. How many times did Snape protect Harry?

65. How many Hogwarts students are accepted each year?

66. Who is Tom Riddle?

67. What is the name of the room Harry uses to teach Dumbledore's Army?

68. Who is the Hufflepuff house ghost?

69. What does the Sorcerer's Stone (Philosopher's Stone) do?

70. Who is Fluffy?

Part 5: Answer 60-70

60. No

61. It is the third and smallest ball used in Quidditch.

62. It is a formal dance held on the evening of Yule.

63. A terrorist group of wizards and witches.

64. 14 times.

65. 1,000 students. Or 250 in each house.

66. A young Lord Voldemort.

67. The Room of Requirement

68. The Fat Friar

69. Transforms any metal to gold and produces the elixer of life

70. Hagrid's three-headed dog

Part 6: Question 71-80

71. What Horcrux is a small golden cup with two finely wrought handles with a badger engraved on the side and a few jewels.

72. Who was the headmaster of Hogwarts when the Chamber of Secrets was opened for the first   time?

73. Slughorn teaches his students that Amortentia smells different to each person. What food does Harry smell?

74. The visitor's entrance to the Ministry of Magic is an abandoned red telephone booth in London. What is the five-digit code you must dial to get in?

75. What power do the dementors have over people?

76. These ingredients: lacewing flies, lecches, powdered Bicorn horn, knotgrass, fluxweed, shredded Boomslang skin, and a bit of the person you want to turn into make what?

77. How many staircases does Hogwarts have?

78. What does the Imperius Curse do?

79. What are the three unforgivable curses?

80. Dumbledore has a scar above his left knee that is a perfect map of what?

Part 6: Answer 71-80

71. Hufflepuff's Cup

72. Armando Dippet

73. Treacle Tart

74. 6-2-4-4-2 (the numbers spell M-A-G-I-C)

75. Power to drain peace, hope and happiness

76. 142

77. Polyjuice Potion

78. Controls the action of another

79. Killing Curse, Cruciatus Curse, and Imperius Curse

80. The London Underground

Quiz 7: Question 81-90

81. What does the Mirror of Erised do?

82. Gryffindor's ghost is Nearly Headless Nick. But what is his full name?

83. Before his second year at Hogwarts, how do the Weasley's save Harry from the Dursley's house?

84. According to the Sorting Hat what qualities does Ravenclaw possess?

85. What school did Viktor Krum go to?

86. What is the name of the book Hermione supposed Voldemort used to learn about Horcruxes?

87. What is Ron Weasley's patronus?

88. What was the name of the brothers who created the Deathly Hallows?

89. Where is the Slytherin common room located?

90. Which creatures pull the carriages that take students from the Hogwarts Express to the Castle?

Part 7: Answer 81-90

81. Show's your heart desire

82. Sir Nicholas de Mimsy-Porpington

83. A flying car

84. Wit and learning

85. Durmstrang Institute

86. Secrets of the Darkest Art

87. Jack Russell Terrier

88. Peverell brothers

89. The dungeons

90. Thestrals

Quiz 8: Question 91-100

91. Where is Azkaban fortress located?

92. What is the name of Albus Dumbledore's brother?

93. Why was the Whomping Willow planted?

94. What type of dragon did Harry face in his first Tri-Wizard Tournament task?

95. What type of Animagus is Rita Skeeter?

96. What is a bezoar?

97. What caused Dumbledore's hand to be blackened and shriveled?

98. What are the first names of Voldemort's parents?

99. Who is the half-blood prince?

100. Which character became a professional Quidditch player?

Part 8: Answer 91-100

91. The North Sea

92. Aberforth

93. To protect Lupin (when he would turn into a werewolf)

94. A Hungari an Horntail

95. A beetle

96. An antidote to poison

97. Marvolo Gaunt's ring (A horcrux)

98. Tom and Merope

99. Severus Snape

100. Ginny Weasley

Part 9: Question 101-110

101. According to the prophecy, who was the other person besides Harry Potter who could possibly vanquish Lord Voldemort?

102. What is the name of the train station that services Hogwarts School?

103. What is it customary for wizard-kind to do before dueling?

104. What was the name of Hermione Granger's pet cat?

105. Who revealed to Lily Potter that she was a witch?

106. What are all of the names of the Weasley children?

107. Who is the founder of the Slug Club?

108. What color are Dobby's eyes?

109. What are the four houses that Hogwart's Students are   sorted into?

110. What are the first names of the Hogwart's founders?

Part 9: Answer 101-110

101. Neville Longbottom

102. Hogsmeade Station

103. Bow

104. Crookshanks

105. Severus Snape

106. Ron Weasley, Ginny Weasley, Bill, Weasley, Percy Weasley, Fred Weasley, Charlie Weasley

107. Horace Slughorn

108. Green

109. Gryffindor, Slytherin, Hufflepuff and Ravenclaw

110. Godric (Gryffindor), Salazar (Slytherin), Helga (Hufflepuff) and Rowena (Ravenclaw)

Part 10: Question 111 -120

111. When Harry finds a message within a counterfeit horcrux of Salazar Slytherin's locket, which initials are signed on the note?

112. What do Hermione's muggle parents do for a living?

113. What does Vernon Dursley's company sell?

114. According to Fred and George Weasley, how many passages are there from Hogwarts to Hogsmeade?

115. Who gave Harry Potter his invisibility cloak?

116. Which department does Arthur Weasley work for at the Ministry of Magic?

117. What is Dolores Umbridge's middle name?

118. What is Harry's wand's core?

119. Which chess piece does Luna Lovegood's house resemble?

120. What does the acronym S.P.E.W. stand for?

Part 10: Answer 111-120

111. R.A.B

112. Dentists

113. Drills

114. 7

115. Albus Dumbledore

116. Misuse of Muggle Artifacts Office

117. Jane

118. Phoenix feather

119. A rook

120. Society for the Promotion of Elfish Welfare

Part 11: Question 121-140

121. Who did Draco Malfoy learn Occlumency from?

122. Why was Fenrir Greyback not allowed to become an official Death Eater?

123. What are the three types of wizard coins in order of value?

124. Which Hogwarts teaching position is cursed?

125. What is the spell to disarm an opponent?

126. What is Neville's toad's name?

127. What color light comes from the killing curse (Avada Kedavra curse)?

128. What does Dumbledore tell Harry he sees in the Mirror of Erised?

130. Who gave Harry his Firebolt broomstick?

131. What do Lupin and Tonks name their son?

132. What plant traps Harry, Ron, and Hermione on their way to get the Philosopher's Stone?

133. What Hogwarts house did Moaning Myrtle belong to?

134. What animal does James Potter transfigure into?

135. What are the last three words in Harry Potter and the Deathly Hallows?

136. Mistletoe is often infested with what magical creature?

137. What condition gives Tonks the ability to transform her features?

138. What does Dumbledore leave Ron in his will?

139. What is the name of Harry Potter's pet owl?

140. Who were the four competitors in Goblet of Fire's Triwizard Tournament?

Part 11: Answer 121-140

121. Bellatrix Lestrange

122. Because he is a werewolf

123. Knut, Sickle, Galleon

124. Defense Against the Dark Arts

125. Expelliarmus

126. Trevor

127. Green

129. Thick wollen socks

130. Sirius Black

131. Edward Remus Lupin

132. Devil's Snare

133. Ravenclaw

134. Stag

135. "All was well."

136. Nargles

137. Metamorphmagus

138. Deluminator

139. Hedwig

140. Fleur Delacour, Viktor Krum, Cedric Diggory, and Harry Potter

Part 12: Question 141-160

141. When is Harry Potter's birthday?

142. Harry wins a vial of what potion from Professor Slughorn?

143. What is the Hogwarts school motto in english?

144. Where did Severus Snape grow up?

145. What did Ginny name the Pygmy Puff that she bought from Weasleys' Wizard Wheezes?

146. Which of Hogwarts professors teaches Transfiguration?

147. What's the name of the fairy-tale book that Dumbledore gives to Hermione in "The Deathly Hallows?"

148. The Potion Puzzle from the Philosopher's Stone is a riddle. You can read the riddle here. Of the seven potions, which one will help you move forward?

149. Fred and George Weasley were born on what day?

150. How does Harry manage to breathe underwater during the second task of the Triwizard Tournament?

151. Who guards the entrance to the Gryffindor common room?

152. A wizard who cannot do magic is known as what?

153. Where does Hermione brew her first batch of Polyjuice Potion?

154. What are the names of Draco Malfoy's two close friends?

155. Who is the Headmistress of Beauxbatons?

156. Which Hogwarts founder did the Sorting Hat originally belong to?

157. What is the name of the dodgy area near Diagon Alley?

158. What does the spell Wingardium Leviosa do?

159. What is the magical creature that can transform itself into a person's worst fear?

160. Who runs Gringott's wizarding bank?

Part 12: Answer 141-160

141. July 31

142. Felix Felicis

143. Never tickle a sleeping dragon

144. Spinner's End

145. Arnold

146. Professor McGonagall

147. The Tales of Beedle theBard

148. The third one

149. April 1st

150. He eats gillyweed

151. The Fat Lady

152. A Squib

153. Moaning Myrtle's Bathroom

154. Crabbe and Goyle

Part 13: Question 161-180

161. What mode of transport does Hagrid use to take Harry to his aunt and uncle's house when he's a baby?

162. What is the name of the giant spider who used to be Hagrid's pet?

163. What is the name of the magical potion that makes people tell the truth?

164. Who is the first one to be petrified in 'Harry Potter and the Chamber of Secrets'?

165. The Dark Mark depicts what two things?

166. What magical device is used to store and review memories?

167. Who originally created the Sorcerer's Stone?

168. What is the name of Voldemort's snake?

169. What color is unicorn blood?

170. Which character has a grandmother who is a Veela (a race of semi-human, semi-magical hominids reminiscent of the Sirens of Greek mythology)?

171. What is renowned wandmaker Ollivander's first name?

172. What is the name for an ordinary object that's been enchanted to teleport people?

173. Where does Hagrid hide his wand?

174. In Harry Potter and the Sorcerer's Stone, into what house is the first student sorted during the Sorting Ceremony?

175. Who was the last person to be sorted before Harry's turn?

176. When Ron, Harry and Hermione started at Hogwarts, Percy Weasley had just been made prefect. What did his parents give him as a reward?

177. What was Nicolas Flamel's most famous creation?

178. Before Rubeus Hagrid began teaching Care of Magical Creatures, who last held that position?

179. What is the lowest grade available on wizarding tests, such as O.W.L.s and N.E.W.T.s?

180. In Prisoner of Azkaban, Harry stays at the Leaky Cauldron and receives help on his History of Magic homework from which Diagon Alley shopkeeper?

Part 13: Answer 161-180

161. Flying motorcycle

162. Aragon

163. Veritaserum

164. Mrs. Norris

165. A skull and a snake

166. Pensieve

167. Nicholas Flamel

168. Nagini

169. Silver

170. Fleur Delacour

171. Garrick

172. Portkey

173. His umbrella

174. Hufflepuff

175. Sally-Anne Perks

176. An owl

177. The Philosopher's Stone

178. Silvanus Kettleburn

179. Troll

180. Florean Fortescue

Part 14: Question 181-200

181. In Goblet of Fire, Harry and Hermione attend the Quidditch World Cup with the Weasleys. Who wins the match?

182. In Half-Blood Prince, Ron accidentally eats a love potion Romilda Vane, a fourth year had intended for Harry. What did she put the potion into?

183. In Prisoner of Azkaban, Ron gets a new wand after his hand-me-down wand was broken the previous year. What wood was the new wand made of?

184. As Prisoner of Azkaban begins, the Weasleys are spending the summer in Egypt visiting Bill. Where did they get the gold to pay for the trip?

185. During one memorable Care of Magical Creatures lesson, the students search for leprechaun gold with the aid of what magical creature?

186. Hermione takes this elective class with Professor Bathsheda Babbling:

187. The Fountain of Magical Brethren, located in the Ministry of Magic, does NOT include a statue of which creature:

188. Hagrid created Blast-Ended Skrewts by breeding which two magical creatures?

189. When Harry first meets Luna Lovegood on the Hogwarts Expressin Order of the Phoenix, she is described as wearing an eccentric outfit, including which accessory?

190. Ron and Harry miss the Hogwarts Express at the beginning of Chamber of Secrets and fly to school in an enchanted car. What kind of car?

191. Molly Weasley lost two brothers in the First Wizarding War. What were their names?

192. What is Fleur Delacour's younger sister's name?

193. Dolores Umbridge was frequently described wearing which distinctive item?

194. After their marriage, Fleur and Bill Weasley set up house together. Where do they live?

195. On Harry's 12th birthday, Dobby the House Elf causes a ruckus and ruins a dinner party the Dursleys are throwing. Who is the guest of honor?

196. What is the first D of the three D's of Apparation?

197. What is Cho Chang's Patronus?

198. Which one of these was NOT a Weasley's Wizard Wheezes creation?

199. How does one find a knarl amid a group of hedgehogs?

200. What is the full name of Gryffindor House's ghost?

Part 14: Answer 181-200

181. Ireland

182. Chocolate Cauldrons

183. Willow

184. Daily Prophet Grand Prize Galleon Draw

185. Nifflers

186. Study of Ancient Runes

187. Veela

188. Manticores and fire crabs

189. A necklace made of Butterbeer caps

190. Ford Anglia

191. Fabian and Gideon

192. Gabrielle

193. A fuzzy pink cardigan

194. Shell Cottage

195. Mr. Mason, a builder

196. Destination

197. Swan

198. Fizzing Whizbees

199. Offer them each a bit of milk

200. Sir Nicholas de Mimsy-Porpington

Part 15: Question 201-220

201. Where is the Slytherin Common Room located?

202. When Harry, Ron and Hermione are captured by Snatchers in Deathly Hallows, who does Hermione claim to be?

203. What does S.P.E.W. stand for?

204. Which one of these was NOT a Gilderoy Lockhart book?

205. Which musical artist does Molly Weasley enjoy playing during the Christmas holidays?

206. Lee Jordan hosts a show on the renegade radio show "Potterwatch" during The Deathly Hallows. What is his pseudonym?

207. In Order of the Phoenix, it's revealed that Hagrid has a giant half-brother. What is his name?

208. What words end the last chapter of Deathly Hallows, before the epilogue?

209. In his first flying lesson, Harry impresses Professor McGonagall with a daring dive. What item was he catching?

210. How does Peter Pettigrew die?

211. Sirius Black, Remus Lupin, Peter Pettigrew and James Potter gave each other nicknames while at Hogwarts. What was Sirius called?

212. Which charm can open a lock?

213. What is Bellatrix Lestrange's husband's name?

214. Voldemort's father was a country squire named Tom Riddle Sr. Who was his mother?

215. In Chamber of Secrets, Professor Binns forgets Hermione's name. What does he call her instead?

216. In Goblet of Fire, the Weasleys surprise the Dursleys with a visit and cause some damage to the house. Which part?

217. After Oliver Wood graduates, who is made captain of the Gryffindor Quidditch team?

218. When Harry receives his O.W.L. results, he's gotten one "Outstanding." In what subject?

219. How many Sickles are in a Galleon?

220. Hagrid gets Harry an owl named Hedwig before he starts at Hogwarts. What kind of owl is she?

Part 15: Answer 201-220

201. In a dungeon under the lake

202. Penelope Clearwater

203. Society for the Promotion of Elfish Welfare

204. Vacations with Vampires

205. Celestina Warbeck

206. River

207. Grawp

208. "I've had enough trouble for a   lifetime."

209. A Remembrall

210. Strangled by his own magical silver hand

211. Padfoot

212. Alohomora

213. Rodolphus

214. Merope Gaunt

215. Miss Grant

216. The electric fireplace

217. Angelina Johnson

218. Defense Against the Dark Arts

119. 17

220. Snowy

Part 16: Question 221-240

221. In Chamber of Secrets, Harry attempts to comfort Nearly Headless Nick after he is rejected from the Headless Hunt by doing what?

222. What form does Ron Weasley's boggart take in their Defense Against the Dark Arts class in Prisoner of Azkaban?

223. What saves Colin Creevey from being killed by the basilisk in Chamber of Secrets?

224. Why would Ron rather go alone to the Yule Ball than with Eloise Midgen?

225. After Hagrid is expelled from Hogwarts, his wand is snapped in half. Where does he keeps the pieces?

226. In his first DADA lesson in the book, Lockhart sets a cage full of what magical creature loose in the classroom?

227. In her singing Valentine to Harry in Chamber of Secrets, Ginny compares Harry's eyes to "fresh pickled toads" and his hair to what?

228. Prior to the Weasley twins opening their joke shop, what wizarding joke store did they frequent in Hogsmeade?

229. In Order of the Phoenix, Hermione communicates meeting times with Dumbledore's Army through imitations of what item?

230. What are Inferi?

231. Which Dumbledore's Army member suffered a jinx after snitching to Umbridge?

232. In Chamber of Secrets, Harry's Herbology class repots Mandrakes. What is the dangerous power of a Mandrake?

233. In Prisoner of Azkaban, the portrait of the Fat Lady guarding Gryffindor Tower is slashed. Who temporarily replaces her?

234. How long is Harry Potter's wand?

235. After Ron begins dating Lavender Brown, who does Hermione attend the Slug Club Christmas party with?

236. In Goblet of Fire, Harry meets Ministry official Ludo Bagman. What is Bagman's role?

237. After the hippogriff Buckbeak is sentenced to death, who is sent to execute him?

238. What is the name of the prep school Dudley Dursley starts attending in the Sorceror's Stone?

239. What is Horace Slughorn's favorite candy?

240. What does Vernon Dursley's company sell?

Part 16: Answer 221-240

221. Agreeing to attend his 500th Deathday Party

222. A giant spider

223. He sees the basilisk through his camera lens.

224. Her nose is off-center.

225. Inside a pink umbrella

226. Cornish pixies

227. A blackboard

228. Zonko's Joke Shop

229. Galleons

230. Animated corpse

231. Marietta Edgecombe

232. Its cry is fatal to those who hear it.

233. A portrait of Sir Cadogan

234. 11 inches

235. Cormac McLaggen

236. Head of the Department of Magical Games and Sports

237. Walden Macnair

238. Smeltings

239. Crystallized pineapple

Part 17: Question 241-260

241. At the beginning of the series, Harry ends up attending Dudley's birthday outing with his aunt, uncle and Dudley's best friend -- what was the friend's name?

242. How many drink bottles containing potion, poison and wine are part of the logic puzzle at the end of Sorcerer's Stone?

243. How do the Weasley twins attempt to fool the Age Line around the Goblet of Fire in order to put their names in for Triwizard Champion?

244. What kind of potion bestows good luck on those who drink it?

245. Who becomes Minister of Magic immediately after Cornelius Fudge?

246. What nickname did Sirius and James give to Severus Snape during their time at Hogwarts?

247. What color was Nymphadora Tonks' hair when Harry first meets her?

248. After Harry and Dudley are attacked by Dementors in Order of the Phoenix, Aunt Petunia receives a Howler. What does it say?

249. What were the Bulgarian National Quidditch Team mascots?

250. Most wands we encounter in the books were made by Ollivander. Who made Viktor Krum's wand?

251. After Harry gets involved in a fight with the Slytherin Quidditch team following a match in Order of the Phoenix, what punishment does Umbridge give him?

252. In Half-Blood Prince, Harry learns that the hippogriff Buckbeak has to be renamed to evade Ministry suspicion. What is his new name?

253. Who gives Katie Bell the cursed necklace in Half-Blood Prince?

254. How is Harry's Nimbus Two Thousand broomstick destroyed?

255. Who is Ginny Weasley's first boyfriend?

256. What is Ron's birthday gift to Harry at the beginning of Prisoner of Azkaban?

257. What is the danger posed by hinkypunks?

258. Where does Hermione find the recipe for the Polyjuice Potion?

259. In which book does Harry first win the Quidditch Cup with the Gryffindor side?

260. Harry nearly dies saving Ginny from the Chamber of Secrets -- what saves his life?

Part 17: Answer 241-260

241. Piers Polkiss

242. 7

243. Aging Potion

244. Felix Felicis

245. Rufus Scrimgeour

246. Snivellus

247. Violet

248. "Hold to your promise." "Remember my last."

249. Veela

250. Gregorovitch

251. A lifetime bans from Quidditch

252. Witherwings

253. Madam Rosmerta

254. The Whomping Willow thrashes it.

255. Michael Corner

256. A Pocket Sneakoscope

257. They lure people into bogs.

258. Most Potente Potions

259. Prisoner of Azkaban

260. Phoenix tears

Part 18: Question 261-280

261. Who was the first master of the Elder Wand?

262. What does the necklace Lavender Brown gave Ron for Christmas in Half-Blood Prince have on it?

263. Who does Harry take to the Slug Club Christmas party?

264. What is the name of the three-headed dog that guards the Sorcerer's Stone?

256. What word does Hermione use to describe the perfume Ron gives her for Christmas in Order of the Phoenix?

266. What color is the Sorcerer's, or Philosopher's, Stone?

267. Goblet of Fire opens at the Riddle House, where Voldemort's father once lived. Outside what village is it located?

268. What is the incantation for a Tickling Charm?

269. Who is the captain of the Holyhead Harpies?

270. What do the Weasley twins use for their final prank before dropping out of Hogwarts?

271. In Half-Blood Prince, Harry meets a vampire at Hogwarts. What is the vampire's name?

272. Dumbledore leaves Harry a Golden Snitch that magically reads "I open at the close." What is inside it?

273. What food did young Tom Riddle give to Professor Slughorn?

274. What is Albus Dumbledore's full name?

275. What is Colin Creevey's brother named?

276. After leaving school, which Quidditch team does Oliver Wood play for?

277. What colour is Ron's favourite Quidditch Team

278. Who was the person to reveal Barty Crouch Jr. as a death eater?

279. What is Harry Potter second born child's full name?

280. What is Madame Maxime's first name?

Part 18: Answer 261-280

261. Antioch Peverell

262. "My Sweetheart"

263. Luna Lovegood

264. Fluffy

265. Unusual

266. Red

267. Little Hangleton

268. Rictusempra

269. Gwenog Jones

270. A Portable Swamp

271. Sanguini

272. The Resurrection Stone

273. Crystalized Pineapple

274. Albus Percival Wulfric Brian Dumbledore

275. Dennis

276. Puddlemere United

277. Orange

278. Igor Karkaroff

279. Albus Severus Potter

280. Olympe

Part 19: Question 281-300

281. Harry Potter's birthday is on _____

282. At the moment of Mad Eye's death, _____ was flying with him.

283. Who is the security guard at the entrance of Gryffindor's Common room?

284. What was used by Dumbledore to light up the Street lights in Privet Drive?

285. What is the occupation of Hermione's parents?

286. Who guided Fleur to the Yule Ball?

287. There is a magical beast, a bright green snake which is hidden in the chamber of Secrets. What is its name?

288. Vernon Dursley was the director of a firm called _____, which made drills.

289. Harry Potters's eyes have a particular color. Which is that color?

290. The name of the prison where Gellert Grindelwald was imprisoned?

291. The actual name of Lord Voldemort is _____

292. In which player position Harry belongs to the Gryffindor Quidditch Team?

293. The platforms from where Hogwarts Express passes are

294. Who defeated Albus Dumbledore in a Global wizarding war in 1945?

295. The birthday of Harry Potter is the same day as that of another one's also. Who is that person?

296. Which mode of Transport was used by Harry and Ron to move to Hogwarts?

297. While doing the Triwizard Tournament's second task, what Harry did for breathing under the water.

298. Which is the middle name of Tom Riddle who is also called Lord Voldemort?

299. Who brought Harry to Hogwarts when he was matured to go there?

300. When Lucius Malfoy took the diary, what did he throw and catch by Dobby which sets Dobby free throughout his lifetime?

Part 19: Answer 281-300

281. July 31

282. Mundungus Fletcher.

283. The Fat Lady.

284. Deluminator.

285. Dentists.

286. Roger Davies.

287. A Basilisk.

288. Grunnings.

289. Green.

290. Nurmengard.

291. Tom Marvolo Riddle.

292. Seeker.

293. Nine and Three-quarters.

294. Grindelwald.

295. J.K. Rowling.

296. flying car.

297. He eats gillyweed.

298. Marvolo.

299. Hagrid.

300. Harry's dirty sock.

Part 20: Question 301-320

301. Who is the headmistress of Beauxbatons Academy of Magic?

302. Which substance is destructive enough to destroy a Horcruxe when exposed to it?

303. Name the book which is given to Harry by Hermione before his first Quidditch match.

304. Death Eaters.

305. What does Professor McGonagall placed in order to guard sorcerer's stone?

306. Who later becomes Lord Voldemort's trusted snake and horcrux?

307. Ronald Weasleyhad a phobia on which insect?

308. Who alone would be able to unseal the Chamber of Secrets?

309. Which was the species of Hagrid's pet dragon?

310. Each year Mrs. Weasley gives a gift to Harry. What is that?

311. The Patronus of Snape was a _____

312. On which occasion twelve-foot troll enter into Hogwart's Academy?

313. Name the Daily which was described throughout the Harry Potter series?

314. Who is the owner of a sorting hat who was one of the founders of Hogwarts?

315. What is the name of the railway station in London to catch the train to Hogwarts where you should stay in between platforms 9 and 10?

316. Who has done the role of Harry Potter in the films?

317. Who is the large dog that accompanied Hagrid in many places?

318. At what age one can join in Hogwarts School of Witchcraft?

319. Who was a British witch who worked as the Flying instructor, Quidditch referee, and coach at Hogwarts School of Witchcraf and Wizardry?

320. Towards the end of the first book 'Harry Potter and the Philosopher's Stone', what gift did Hagrid give to Harry?

Part 20: Answer 301-320

301. Madame Maxime.

302. Basilisk venom.

303. Quidditch through the Ages.

304. Name the Godfather of Harry Potter?

305. Wizarding Chess.

306. Nagini.

307. Spiders.

308. The Heir of Slytherin.

309. Norwegian Ridgeback.

310. A New Sweater.

311. Doe.

312. Halloween.

313. Daily Prophet.

314. Godric Gryffindor.

315. King's Cross.

316. Daniel Radcliffe.

317. Fang.

318. 11.

319. Madam Rolanda Hooch.

320.   A photo album of his parents.

Part 21: Question 321-340

321. Who are the parents of Ron?

322. On Dudley's birthday at the zoo, unknowingly using underage magic Harry made the glass of a snake's cage vanish. What is its name?

323. Name the phoenix which was Albus Dumbledore's animal companion and defender.

324. Name the extremely unsocial ghost of Slytherin who is the only one can control Peeves?

325. Who was Harry's captain in Slytherin in his first Quidditch match?

326. There is a female dragon Nobert in Harry Potter. What is its species?

327. Name the person who usually referred to as Wormtail or Scabbers?

328. Name the category who was born into a wizarding family but hasn't got any magic powers?

329. Which animal attacked Ron's father when Harry had an intense dream?

330. Robert portrayed which character in the film adaptation of Harry Potter and the Goblet of Fire in 2005?

331. Name the magical potion that makes the drinker lucky for a period of time, during which everything they attempt will be successful in Harry Potter and the Half-Blood Prince'

332. Vernon Dursley had his own office on the _____ floor of his drill company, Grunnings.

333. Which character in Harry Potter carries a camera always with him at Hogwarts?

334. _____is the password given to the fat lady to enter into Gryffindor tower

335. Harry's best friends are _____and ____

336. The role of Professor McGonagall was done in the movies by
_____

337. In which House did Sorting hat want to include Harry?

338. Who was appointed as the guards of Azkaban prison by The Ministry of Magic?

339. Who is Harry's Father?

340. To which school Harry has been planning to go in the fall, before getting his invitation to Hogwarts school?

Part 21: Answer 321-340

321. Molly and Arthur Weasley.

322. Boa Constrictor.

323. Fawkes.

324. The Bloody Baron.

325. Marcus Flint.

326. Norwegian Ridge back.

327. Peter Pettigrew.

328. Squib.

329. A snake   330. Cedric Diggory.

331. Felix Felicis.

332. 9th.

333. Colin Creevey.

334. Pig Snout.

335. Hermione and Ron.

336. Maggie Smith.

337. Slytherin.

338. Dementors.

339. James Potter.

340. Stonewall.

Part 22: Question 341-360

341. Who kisses Harry after DA lesson in Harry Potter and the Order of the Phoenix'?

342. What was Hermione's weapon to escape from Devil's Snare plant?

343. Name the mother of Severus Snape, who was a pure-blooded witch

344. _____ was the street address of the home owned by Vernon and Petunia Dursley

345. In the first book, which flavor ice cream is eating by Harry at the zoo?

346. What is the name of Hagrid's pet, a giant spider?

347. Date of birth of Harry Potter is on

348. What is the name of the fictitious author, which is also the pen name of JK Rowling, who wrote the book Fantastic Beasts and Where to find them'?

349. Name the place where Harry was born?

350. ____ became a Chaser on the Gryffindor Quidditch team by or before her third year.

351. _____ was the name of Harry's mother's maid

352. Which shade did Ron change Scabbers into?

353. Which job did Harry acquire when he grew up?

354. What was the former name of Professor Sprout?

355. Name the person who keeps the Potter family's secret.

356. Gryffindor quidditch team captain is _____

357. The place where Harry met with Quirinus Quirrell for the first time is.

358. Who made Sorcerer's stone, an object capable of turning metal into gold and granting immortality with its Elixir of Life?

359. Harry usually plays a game using the cupboard as _____ below the stairs.

360. In which place Harry realized he can talk with the snakes?

Part 22: Answer 341-360

341. Cho Chang.

342. Fire.

343. Eileen.

344. 4 Privet Drive.

345. Lemon Ice Pop.

346. Aragog.

347. 31st of July 1980.

348. Newt Scamander.

349. Godric's Hollow.

350. Angelina Johnson.

351. Evans.

352. Yellow.

353. Head of the Auror Office.

354. Pomona.

355. Peter Pettigrew.

356. Oliver Wood.

357. The Leaky Cauldron.

358. Nicholas Flamel.

359. Toy Soldiers.

360. At the Zoo.

Part 23: Question 361-380

361. Who are the police force, and sometimes work as intelligence agents and have the authority to arrest malefactors like Death Eaters in the wizard world?

362. Which tree's wood is used to make Harry's magic wand?

363. Which color represents Slytherin houses?

364. To which school Harry planned to go before he decided to go to Hogwarts?

365. Harry passed out for ___ days after finding the sorcerer's stone?

366. In his first quidditch match, Harry's team was against which House

367. Name the person who put Harry's name in the Goblet of Fire?

368. Hogwarts School of Witchcraft and Wizardry has a very loyal flock of _____ used mainly to pull the carriages that lead elder students from Hogsmeade station to the gates of the Castle.

369. The colors which represent Ravenclaw house are _____ and _____

370. Name the first captain of Harry in quidditch match.

371. What gift did grandmother give Neville in his first year at Hogwarts?

372. Which is the magical device, a stone basin, used to save and review memories?

373. Prefects' Bathroom's door is left to whose statue?

374. Who is the producer of the philosopher's stone?

375. The place where Vernon Dursley works?

376. Fist name of Macnair, who is a death eater too?

377. Professor Quirrell's original name is

378. Name the warden of the orphanage from where Voldemort came from?

379. Which actor plays Harry Potter?

380. Who was Harry Potter's first crush?

Part 23: Answer 361-380

361. Aurors.

362. Holly.

363. Green and silver.

364. Stonewall High.

365. 3.

366. Slytherin.

367. Barty Crouch, Jr.

368. Thestrals.

369. Blue and Bronze.

370. Oliver Wood.

371. A Remembrall.

372. Pensieve.

373. Boris the Bewildered.

374. Nicolas Flamel.

375. Grunnings.

376. Walden.

377. Quirinus.

378. Mrs. Cole

379. Daniel Radcliffe

380. Cho Chang

Part 24: Question 381-400

381. What shape does Harry's Patronus take?

382. Where in their house did the Dursleys make Harry sleep when he was a child?

383. What platform is used for the Hogwarts Express?

384. What is the name of Harry's cousin?

385. What was Harry's first broomstick?

386. What is the name of the wizarding world's newspaper?

387. Where does the Dursley family live?

388. Which schoolhouse is Harry sorted into?

389. Who teaches potions at Hogwarts?

390. What shape is Harry's scar?

391. What object is Professor Slughorn disguised as when Harry first meets him?

392. Who is the 'Prisoner of Azkaban'?

393. Where do Harry and Cho share their first kiss?

394. What creatures guard Azkaban?

395. What is the name of Dumbledore's phoenix?

396. What was the name of Ron's pet rat?

397. What did the boggart turn into when Parvati Patil faced it?

398. What nickname is used for civilians outside of the wizarding world?

399. Who is the caretaker at Hogwarts?

400. How did the Dursleys explain the death of Harry's parents to him?

Part 24: Answer 381-400

381. A stag

382. In the cupboard under the stairs

383. 9 3/4

384. Dudley

385. Nimbus 2000

386. The Daily Prophet

387. 4 Privet Drive

388. Gryffindor

389. Professor Snape

390. Lightning bolt

391. An armchair

392. Sirius Black

393. In the room of Requirement

394. Dementors

395. Fawkes

396. Scabbers

397. A Snake

398. Muggles

399. Argus Filch

400. They said his parents died in a car crash